NATIONAL GEOGRAPHIC

Holiday 1 Explorer

English for short courses

T0349596

HEINLE

CENGAGE Learning

Australia • Brazil • Japan • Korea • Mexico • Singapore • Spain • United Kingdom • United States

Welcome to Holiday Explorer!

This book will help you to learn, practise and remember English ... and it's easy to use!

You will find the following in each of the 6 units:

- *Vocabulary* an entertaining introduction to new words
- *Dialogue* language in interesting situations
- *Grammar* lots of revision and practice
- *Functions* useful language for the daily lives of young people
- *Skills* practise new language and learn about culture
- *Waow!* a fun magazine just for you

Remember!

- Whenever you see this symbol  use the audio CD.
- Turn to the grammar reference section at the back of the book when you need extra help.
- Complete the word list at the back of the book and remember all the words you learn.

CRACK THE CODE

Each unit finishes with a code cracking activity. Solve the puzzles and find hidden words.

So, what are you waiting for?

Contents

Friends and family

Vocabulary

① Complete the family tree

Look at the words below and write them under the pictures of the family and friends to show their relationship to Damien.

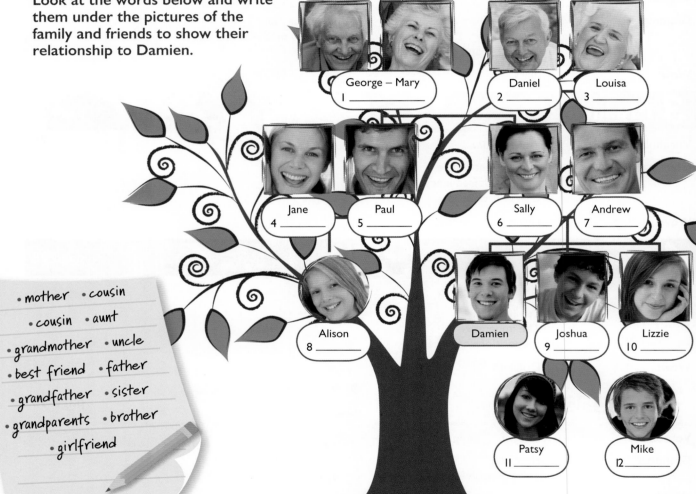

George – Mary
1 _____

Daniel
2 _____

Louisa
3 _____

Jane
4 _____

Paul
5 _____

Sally
6 _____

Andrew
7 _____

Alison
8 _____

Damien

Joshua
9 _____

Lizzie
10 _____

Patsy
11 _____

Mike
12 _____

- mother • cousin
- cousin • aunt
- grandmother • uncle
- best friend • father
- grandfather • sister
- grandparents • brother
- girlfriend

② Write

How are these people related to Damien? Unscramble the words.

1   Mary: ehntgoamrrd _____

2   Sally: ehrmto _____

3   Mike: sbte nedfir _____

4   George: arhredgtafn _____

5   Sally and Andrew: tnepsra _____

③ Write

How are these people related to Damien? Write full sentences.

1   Patsy: *Patsy is his friend.*

2   Lizzie: _____

3   Daniel and Louisa: _____

4   Tom and Alison: _____

5   Jane: _____

That's my grandmother

④ Listen and read

Listen to this conversation and follow it in your book.

Patsy	What's that, Damien?
Damien	It's a photo of my family.
Patsy	Really? Oh, it's a birthday party! Who's that woman with the cake?
Damien	That's my grandmother. Her name's Louisa and she's 75. And that's my other grandmother. Her name's Mary. The two men on the right are my grandfathers.
Patsy	Ahh! It's a really happy photo! Is that your aunt?
Damien	Yes, it is. That's Aunt Jane … and that's Uncle Paul. He's a doctor and she's a teacher. They're from Glasgow.
Patsy	And who are the two children?
Damien	They're my cousins, Tom and Alison.
Patsy	Are they twins?
Damien	No, they're not. They're nine and ten.
Patsy	And who is that?
Damien	That's their dog, Meg!
Patsy	She's lovely! You're a big family!
Damien	Yes, we are!

⑤ Comprehension

Are the statements true (T) or false (F)? Correct the false statements.

1 Louisa is 85 years old. _____

_____

2 Andrew is his uncle. _____

_____

3 Jane is a doctor. _____

_____

4 Tom and Alison are brother and sister.

_____

5 They are a small family. _____

_____

⑥ Write

Write sentences about you.

1 How old are you?

I'm _____

2 Where are you from?

_____

3 Who is your best friend?

_____

4 What is the name of your school?

_____

5 What is your favourite sport?

_____

Grammar

Personal pronouns and possessive adjectives

① Complete the table.

personal pronouns	possessive adjectives
1 _____	my
you	2 _____
3 _____	his
she	4 _____
5 _____	its
we	6 _____
7 _____	your
they	8 _____

② Complete the sentences with a personal pronoun.

1 Hi, _____'m Sonia.

2 My grandmother is 89 – _____'s very old.

3 Tommy and Vic are in my class. _____ are very nice.

4 Lisa and I are cousins. _____ are both 13 years old.

5 You and Nadia are in class 1F. _____ are classmates.

③ Complete the text with the correct personal pronouns.

Hi, I'm Sean and this is 1 _____my_____ family. Mum is a doctor and 2 _____ name is Victoria. Dad is a teacher and 3 _____ name is Ben. My grandparents aren't in this photo but 4 _____ names are John and Patricia. Oh, and there's also 5 _____ cat, Saffron. She's lovely!

Regular plurals

④ Complete the table.

singular	plural
friend	1 _____
classmate	2 _____

Variations in spelling

⑤ Complete the table.

singular	plural
bus	1 _____
kiss	2 _____
watch	3 _____
brush	4 _____
box	5 _____
day	6 _____
baby	7 _____

Irregular plurals

⑥ Complete the table.

singular	plural
man	1 _____
woman	2 _____
child	3 _____
mouse	4 _____
fish	5 _____

⑦ Write the plural of these words.

1 sister _____
2 country _____
3 class _____
4 fox _____
5 mother _____
6 mouse _____

Need help? Go to page 52!

The verb *be*

⑧ Complete the table.

affirmative		negative		question	short answers
I am	I'm	I am not	I'm not	Am I?	Yes, you are / No, you're not.
you are	you're	you are not	you aren't	_____ you?	Yes, I _____ / No, I'm not.
he _____	he _____	he _____	he _____	_____ he?	Yes, he _____ / No, he _____ .
she _____	she _____	she _____	she _____	_____ she?	Yes, she _____ /
it _____	it _____	it is _____	it isn't	_____ it?	No, she _____ .
we _____	we _____	we are not	we _____	_____ we?	Yes, it _____ / No, it _____ .
you _____	you _____	you _____	you _____	_____ you?	Yes, we _____ / No, we _____ .
they _____	they _____	they _____	they _____	_____ they?	Yes, you _____ /
					No, you _____ .
					Yes, they _____ /
					No, they _____ .

⑨ Complete the dialogue with the correct forms of the verb *be*.

Emily   Hi! ¹ ___*I'm*___ Emily.

Penny   Hi, Emily. I ² _____ Penny.

Emily   ³ _____ you in 1F?

Penny   No, I ⁴ _____ not. I ⁵ _____ in 1G.

Emily   My friends Barbara and Jim ⁶ _____ in 1G.

Penny   That ⁷ _____ right. We ⁸ _____ all in the same class. But my twin cousins, Laura and Beth, ⁹ _____ in your class.

Emily   ¹⁰ _____ they your cousins? They ¹¹ _____ very nice. I really like them.

Penny   Oh, that's the bell! It ¹² _____ eight o'clock. Bye, Emily.

Emily   Bye, Penny.

I am Emily.

I am Penny.

Question words

⑩ Complete the questions with *who*, *what*, *how* or *where*.

1   _____ is your name?

  Andrea.

2   _____ is your English teacher?

  Mr Judds.

3   _____ is Venice?

  In Italy.

4   _____ old is Rachel?

  She's 14.

⑪ Match the questions to the answers.

1	Where is Paris?	a	It's my new mobile phone.
2	What's this?	b	I'm in class.
3	Who is Ken?	c	I'm fine.
4	Who are they?	d	He's my brother.
5	Where are you?	e	They are my cousins.
6	How are you?	f	It's in France.

Need help? Go to page 52!

Functions

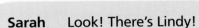

Introducing people

① **Read and listen.**

Sarah	Look! There's Lindy!
Jack	Where?
Sarah	There! Outside the Odeon Cinema.
Lindy	Hello, Sarah!
Sarah	Hi, Lindy. This is my little brother, Jack.
Lindy	Hi Jack, nice to meet you.
Jack	Hello, Lindy. Nice to meet you, too.
Lindy	So how old are you, Jack?
Jack	I'm eleven. I'm in the first year at secondary school.
Lindy	I see. Three years below Sarah and me.
Jack	Yes, that's right.
Sarah	OK. Let's go to the Tip-Top café – I'm really thirsty.
Lindy	Good idea, Sarah. It's a cool place.
Jack	Yes, and I'm hungry!
Sarah	You're always hungry!

② **Read**

Tick (✓) the correct sentences.

1 a ◯ Lindy and Jack are brother and sister.

 b ◯ Sarah and Jack are brother and sister.

2 a ◯ Lindy is outside the Odeon Cinema.

 b ◯ Lindy is outside the Odeon Theatre.

3 a ◯ Jack, Sarah and Lindy are all at secondary school.

 b ◯ Only Jack is at secondary school.

4 a ◯ Jack and Sarah are in the same year at school.

 b ◯ Lindy and Sarah are in the same year at school.

5 a ◯ Sarah is hungry.

 b ◯ Jack is hungry.

③ **Write**

Complete the dialogue.

Lindy	¹ _____ , Sarah! How are you?
Sarah	I'm very well, thanks. ² _____ my friend Paul.
Lindy	Nice to meet you, Paul.
Paul	³ _____ .
Lindy	So, where are you from?
Paul	⁴ _____ London.
Lindy	Oh, that's great.
Paul	⁵ _____ ?
Lindy	I'm from Blackdean, in the west of England. How old are you?
Paul	⁶ _____ .
Lindy	Really? I'm fourteen too!

Skills

① Read

Read the text about Jenny. How many brothers and sisters has she got?

Hi, everybody. My name's Jenny and I'm 15 years old. I'm from Blackpool, a town in the north of England. My surname is Bertolli, and my family is from Italy – my grandfather is from Trento. My best friends are Anna and Kate. We are all in the same class at school.

Music and biology are my favourite subjects at school. My family is very small – just my parents, my brother, Peter, and me. My Italian grandfather, Aldo, lives with us, too. My father is a teacher at a primary school, and my mother is a doctor at Blackpool Hospital. Peter is little – he's only five. He is a big problem when my friends are at our house – he's very curious about what we say and do!

② Comprehension

Read the text about Jenny again and decide if these statements are true (T) or false (F). Correct the false statements.

1 Jenny is fourteen years old. _____
   _____

2 She is from Blackpool. _____
   _____

3 Her family is from Italy. _____
   _____

4 Her family is very big. _____
   _____

③ Listen

Listen to the questions about Jenny and her family and write the answers.

1 _____
2 _____
3 _____
4 _____
5 _____

④ Write

Write a short paragraph about yourself. Use the text above to help you. Remember to include the following points:

✓ your surname
✓ your age
✓ where you are from
✓ the name of your best friend(s)
✓ your favourite school subject
✓ members of your family

Hello, everybody! My name's

Seasons

① Read

Read the texts and complete the gaps with the words in the box.

| autumn | the USA | cold | animals |

In winter in Britain the days are very short and there isn't a lot of light. The weather is ¹ _____ but the temperatures do not often go below 0°C. Young people are very happy when it snows. Schools often close for the day and the students can play outside on sledges.

Spring is the season of new life. The countryside is full of lots of young ² _____ and colourful flowers. The weather also changes a lot. It is possible to have rain, sun, wind and even snow – all in one day! People never know what clothes to wear!

In summer the weather is usually hot and the days are long. It is sunny and the temperatures are high. But in Britain this is not always true. It can rain and be cold. Lots of British people go on holiday abroad in July and August. Popular destinations are Spain, France and Italy, but sometimes they go to more exotic places like ³ _____ , Thailand or Australia!

The countryside changes again in ⁴ _____ . The leaves on the trees become lots of different colours – orange, yellow, red and brown. It's beautiful! A very popular festival in Britain in October is Halloween. Lots of children wear costumes and go to Halloween parties.

WORD LIST

light	_____	sledges	_____	colourful	_____	change	_____
below	_____	countryside	_____	wear	_____	become	_____
outside	_____	full of	_____	abroad	_____	leaves	_____

② Comprehension

Are the statements true (T) or false (F). Correct the false statements.

1 There is a lot of light in winter. _____

_____

2 Young people are very sad when it snows. _____

_____

3 In spring the weather can change a lot. _____

_____

4 Spain, France and Poland are popular holiday destinations in Britain.

_____

The shortest day of the year is 21st December. The longest day of the year is 21st June.

③ Write

Match the words to the correct season.

| New Year's Day | long holidays | Valentine's Day | May Day | my birthday |

winter

summer

spring

autumn

_____   _____   _____   _____

CRACK THE CODE

④ **Can you solve this little puzzle? Read the words with a mirror and then complete the crossword. Two new words will appear!**

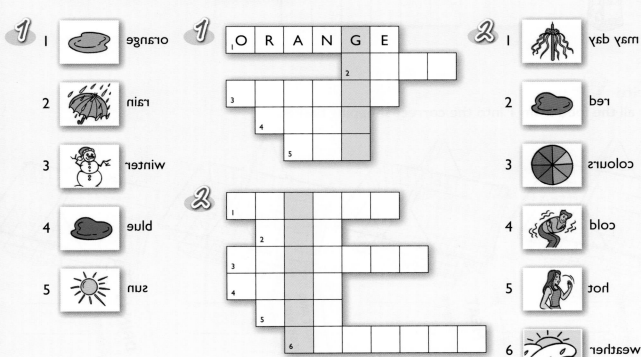

1

1 orange

2 rain

3 winter

4 blue

5 sun

1
```
O R A N G E
      2
3
  4
    5
```

2
```
  1
 2
 3
4
  5
6
```

2

1 may day

2 red

3 colours

4 cold

5 hot

6 weather

2

Vocabulary

① Crossword
Complete the crossword.

Down

1
2
4
5
6
7

Across

3
4
8
9

② Write
Put all the food from 1 into the correct shopping basket.

DAIRY — *butter* _____

MEAT _____

FRUIT AND VEGETABLES _____

DRINKS _____

Is there any milk?

③ Listen and read

Listen to this dialogue and follow it in your book.

Mother	Right. What's in the fridge, Tina? Is there any milk?
Tina	Yes, there's one bottle.
Mother	OK. And what about eggs? Are there any eggs?
Tina	Yes, there are, but only two in the box.
Mother	Cheese?
Tina	Yes, there's some cheese.
Mother	How much is there?
Tina	About 100 grams.
Mother	Right. Is there any orange juice?
Tina	There's half a carton.
Mother	And how much butter is there?
Tina	There's a new packet.
Mother	Good. Are there any vegetables?
Tina	Let's see … there are some carrots and some potatoes.
Mother	How many potatoes are there?
Tina	Erm … six large ones.
Mother	OK. That's it … oh wait, is there any meat?
Tina	I don't think so … no, there isn't any.
Mother	Right. OK, close the fridge. Here's the list … let's go shopping!

④ Comprehension

Read the dialogue again. Tick (✓) the correct sentences.

1 a ◯ There are three bottles of milk in the fridge.

  b ◯ There is one bottle of milk in the fridge.

2 a ◯ There is a new packet of butter.

  b ◯ There is no butter.

3 a ◯ There are some carrots and potatoes.

  b ◯ There are some carrots and broccoli.

4 a ◯ There is some meat.

  b ◯ There is no meat.

⑤ Write

Unscramble the food words.

1 kmil _____ *milk* _____

2 ttbeur _____

3 tgaselebve _____

4 srrctao _____

5 eeehsc _____

6 aonreg cijeu _____

7 soptateo _____

8 etma _____

Grammar

There is / There are

1 Complete the table.

	affirmative	negative	interrogative	short answer
singular	there is (there's)	there [1] _____ (there isn't)	Is there …?	Yes, there [2] _____ . No, there [3] _____ .
plural	there [4] _____ .	there are not (there [5] _____)	[6] _____ there …?	Yes, there [7] _____ . No, there [8] _____ .

a / an

2 Choose the correct words to complete these sentences.

1 *a* + word that begins with a vowel / consonant sound.

2 *an* + word that begins with a vowel / consonant sound.

3 Write *a* or *an*.

an orange   _____ banana   _____ apple   _____ chicken

Countable and uncountable nouns

4 Choose the correct words to complete these sentences.

1 apple, orange, biscuit, egg are countable / uncountable words.

2 milk, coffee, water, wine are countable / uncountable words.

5 Put these food items into the correct basket.

carrot   bread   pear   sandwich   meat   tomato   ~~apple~~   cheese   ~~rice~~   salt

countable

_____apple_____
_____
_____
_____
_____

uncountable

_____rice_____
_____
_____
_____
_____

Need help? Go to page 53!

some / any

⑥ Complete the table.

	affirmative	negative	question	short answer
singular countable	There is a carrot.	There isn't an apple.	Is there an orange?	
singular uncountable	There is ¹ _____ cheese.	There isn't ² _____ sugar.	Is there ³ _____ coffee?	Yes, there is. No, there isn't.
plural	There are ⁴ _____ chips.	There aren't ⁵ _____ tomatoes.	Are there ⁶ _____ biscuits?	Yes, there are. No, there aren't.

⑦ Look at the picture and complete the questions and answers with *a/an*, *some* or *any*.

1 Is there _____*a*_____ bottle of milk?
2 Yes, _*there is.*_____
3 Is there _____ apple?
4 No, _____
5 Is there _____ cheese?
6 Yes, _____
7 Is there _____ butter?
8 No, _____
9 Are there _____ eggs?
10 No, _____
11 Are there _____ carrots?
12 Yes, _____

⑧ What else is there in the picture?

1 _There is some water._____
2 _____

How much / How many...?

⑨ Complete the rules.

1 _____ is used with uncountable nouns.
2 _____ is used with countable nouns.

⑩ Complete the questions with *how much* or *how many*.

1 _How much___ sugar?
   One cup.
2 _____ cakes?
   Two.
3 _____ milk?
   Two litres.

Need help? Go to page 53!

Functions

Ordering food and drink

① Listen and read 🔘⁵
Listen to the dialogue and follow it
in your book.

Kate	Here we are!
Peter	I'm ready for a drink! Is there any pineapple juice?
Kate	No, there isn't … but there's a pineapple smoothie.
Peter	Great. One pineapple smoothie for me, please.
Waitress	Certainly. Anything to eat?
Peter	Yes, please … some chocolate cake, please!
Waitress	Sure. What about you, dear?
Kate	A glass of apple juice for me, please.
Waitress	Right. And for you? What would you like?
Diane	Erm … iced tea, please. Thanks.
Waitress	Anything to eat?
Diane	Yes, some apple pie, please, with ice cream! I'm hungry! How much is that altogether?
Waitress	Erm … that's £7.35, please.
Diane	Here's £10.
Waitress	Thank you … and £2.65 for you.
Diane	Thanks.

② Comprehension
What do Peter, Kate and Diane order?

Peter	Kate	Diane
_____	_____	_____
_____		

③ Reorder
Put the dialogues in the correct order.

1 a Thank you. ◯

   b No, there isn't. But there is some apple pie. ◯

   c OK. Here you are. ◯

   d Hello. Is there any apple juice, please? ◯

   e A bottle of water and some apple pie then, please! ◯

2 a A hot chocolate, please. ◯

   b Thank you … and here's your change. ◯

   c That's £1.50. ◯

   d What would you like? ◯

   e Here's £5. ◯

Read and write

④ Read the menu and write a similar dialogue between you and a waitress. Use the dialogue above to help you.

TIP-TOP CAFÉ MENU

DRINKS		COLD FOOD	
Pot of tea	£1.20	Sandwiches (with salad):	
Cup of coffee	£1.50	Tuna	£1.90
Hot chocolate	£1.10	Cheese	£1.70
Apple juice	90p	Egg	£1.40
Pineapple juice	£1.00		
Mineral water	£1.00	DESSERTS	
		Ice cream	£1.70
HOT FOOD		Apple pie	£1.50
Fish & chips	£5.50	Fruit cake	£1.40
Beans & chips	£4.00	Chocolate cake	£1.25
Egg & chips	£3.50		

You	¹ _____
Waitress	Certainly. Anything to eat?
You	² _____
Waitress	Here you are, dear.
You	³ _____
Waitress	It's £ ⁴ _____ , please.
You	⁵ _____
Waitress	Thank you very much.

Skills

① Read

Read this text and find three things that British people eat.

Food changes

fruit smoothie

What is one of the favourite dishes in Britain today? It isn't only fish and chips. It's also curry. Curry is meat or vegetables in a spicy sauce and you usually eat it with some rice. It's a dish from India and Thailand. And what is their favourite hot drink at breakfast? It isn't only the famous cup of tea. Many people also drink coffee and in the streets there are coffee shops everywhere. Fruit smoothies are very popular now. You can have a smoothie with lots of different fruit, like mango and banana together!

In the supermarkets, you can buy fruit and vegetables from all over the world. People eat food from all over the world. And many British people now eat a lot of pasta, too!

 curry
 coffee shop
 coffee

② Comprehension

Answer the questions.

1 What is the favourite British food now?

_____

2 Where is curry from?

_____

3 Is tea the only hot drink for breakfast in Britain today?

_____

4 Do many British people now eat pasta?

_____

③ Listen 🎵⑥

Listen to some people ordering their food and drinks at the Tip-Top Café. Tick (✓) what each person orders.

1 The boy orders ...
   a fish and chips and an iced tea. ◯
   b fish and chips and a cup of coffee. ◯
   c eggs and a cup of coffee. ◯

2 The mother orders ...
   a a cup of coffee and a cheese sandwich. ◯
   b an iced tea and a cheese sandwich. ◯
   c a cup of coffee and some apple pie. ◯

3 The father orders ...
   a a pot of tea and some fruit cake. ◯
   b a glass of water and a slice of fruit cake. ◯
   c a glass of water and a slice of apple pie. ◯

④ Write

Write a paragraph about what is popular to eat and drink in your country.

🕐 For breakfast: _____
_____

🕐 For lunch: _____
_____

🕐 For dinner: _____
_____

⑤ Write

Write an email to a British friend about your favourite food. Remember to include:

✓ Your favourite food
✓ Your favourite drink
✓ Ask Kate about her favourite food and drink

@ kate.jones@mymail.com

Dear Kate,
How are you?
_____
_____
_____

Write soon!
Love _____

MARS

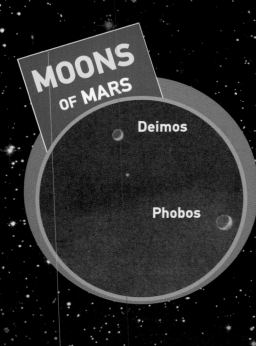

MOONS OF MARS

Deimos

Phobos

 Read

Read the text and complete the sentences with the words in the box.

| any | small | hot | spring | colour |

1 **Q** Is the weather on Mars cold or [1]_____ ?

A It's very cold! The normal temperature is -63°C but it can be warmer, sometimes even 20°C.

2 **Q** How many seasons are there on Mars?

A There are four seasons on Mars: winter, [2]_____ , summer and autumn. But the seasons on Mars are much longer – summer on Mars is six months!

3 **Q** How many moons has Mars got?

A Mars has got two moons. Their names are Phobos and Deimos. They are very [3]_____ ! Phobos is 20 kilometres wide and Deimos only 12 kilometres.

4 **Q** What is another name for Mars?

A Some people call Mars the Red Planet because of its [4]_____ .

5 **Q** Are there any mountains on Mars?

A Yes, there are many. The highest is a volcano called Olympus Mons. It's very tall, about 27 kilometres, but it isn't active.

6 **Q** Is there [5]_____ water on Mars?

A Yes, there is but it is so cold that it is all ice!

7 **Q** How many days are there in a year on Mars?

A There are 687 days in a year on Mars, that's almost two years for us! A day on Mars is similar to our day – it's 24 hours and 37 minutes.

8 **Q** So is there life on Mars?

A We don't know! Scientists are looking for life on Mars but the truth is they still aren't sure!

WORD LIST

moon	_____	similar to	_____	because of	_____
twenty-two	_____	mountains	_____	ice	_____
kilometres wide	_____	volcano	_____	scientists	_____

② Comprehension

Read the text on page 18 again and complete
the table about Mars.

WOW!

Earth is twice the size
of Mars!

FACTSHEET		
Seasons	4	1 _____
Days in a year	365	2 _____
Hours in a day	23 hours, 56 minutes	3 _____
Number of moons	1	4 _____
Name of moon(s)	The Moon	5 _____ 6 _____
Highest mountain	Mount Everest	7 _____
Is there life?	Yes!	8 _____

CRACK THE CODE

③ Help the Martians find their spaceships! Clue: match the opposite words.

1 hot 2 short 3 summer 4 big 5 day tall cold night winter small

④ Now complete the table with the opposite words and crack the code.

	SPACESHIP					
1	C	O	L	D		
2						
3						
4						
5						

The number is: _____ .

My life

3

Vocabulary

① Match

Look at the pictures of what Duncan does on Monday mornings.
Match the sentences to the correct pictures.

1   He leaves the house.   ◯   4   He arrives at school.   ◯   7 He writes emails.   ◯

2   He has a maths lesson.   ◯   5   He gets up.   ◯   8 He eats breakfast.   ◯

3   He has a shower.   ◯   6   He has lunch.   ◯   9 He takes the bus.   ◯

a   b   c   d   e   f   g   h   i

② Write

Write the words from exercise 1 in the correct order next to the times.

1   _He gets up_ at seven o'clock.

2   _____ at quarter past seven.

3   _____ at half past seven.

4   _____ at eight o'clock.

5   _____ at quarter past eight.

6   _____ at quarter to nine.

7   _____ at half past nine.

8   _____ at one o'clock.

9   _____ at five o'clock.

What do you do at the weekends?

③ Listen and read ⑦

Listen to this dialogue and follow
it in your book.

Duncan	What do you usually do at the weekends, Peter?
Peter	Well, I always get up late on Saturday mornings. I have lunch then I meet my friends.
Duncan	Where do you meet them?
Peter	I usually meet them in town. We sometimes go and look at new CDs and computer games.
Duncan	And in the evenings?
Peter	It depends. Sometimes I stay at home and watch TV. We sometimes go to the cinema too.
Duncan	Cool. And on Sundays?
Peter	Well, I play rugby in the winter, so I always get up early.
Duncan	Who do you play for?
Peter	Blackdean Under 13s. Then in the afternoons I usually visit my granddad. He lives near us, so I see him, too.
Duncan	And when do you do your homework?
Peter	I do it on the school bus on Monday morning!
Duncan	Really? Why do you do it on the bus?
Peter	I'm only joking! I never do it on the bus! I always do it on Sunday evenings because I'm so busy all weekend.

WORD LIST

a forward _____

I'm only joking! _____

④ Comprehension

Answer the questions.

1 Does Peter always get up late on Saturday mornings?

_____

2 What does Peter look at in town?

_____

3 Who lives near Peter?

_____

4 Why does he do his homework on Sunday evenings?

_____

⑤ Find the sentence

There is one word in each line.
Find the words to make a sentence.

B	D	U	N	C	A	N	N	G	J	K
R	T	Y	U	O	O	F	T	E	N	L
G	O	E	S	T	A	A	S	D	F	J
O	M	T	F	G	Y	U	I	T	O	K
Q	X	Y	G	T	H	E	B	N	M	K
F	R	I	T	J	C	I	N	E	M	A
W	I	T	H	K	L	G	N	R	R	Y
W	P	P	A	T	S	Y	A	G	N	M
T	T	I	N	H	S	M	O	N	F	O
Y	F	R	I	D	A	Y	T	Y	J	K
H	N	I	G	H	T	S	F	D	S	A

Write the sentence here:

_____

Grammar

The present simple (affirmative)

① Complete the table.

affirmative		
I learn	I [1] _____	I wash
you [2] _____	you go	you [3] _____
he learns	he [4] _____	he [5] _____
she [6] _____	she [7] _____	she [8] _____
it [9] _____	it [10] _____	it [11] _____
we [12] _____	we go	we [13] _____
you [14] _____	you [15] _____	you wash
they [16] _____	they [17] _____	they [18] _____

② Look at the pictures and complete the sentences with the correct form of the verbs in the box.

~~study~~   play   finish   do

1 He ___studies___ English at school.

2 Mum _____ work at 6 o'clock.

3 They _____ tennis at the club.

4 Dad _____ the washing up on Saturdays.

The present simple (negative)

③ Complete the table.

negative	
I do not eat	I don't eat
you [1] _____ eat	you don't eat
he [2] _____ eat	he doesn't eat
she [3] _____ eat	she doesn't eat
it does not eat	it [4] _____ eat
we do not eat	we [5] _____ eat
you [6] _____ eat	you don't eat
they [7] _____ eat	they don't eat

④ Match the words to make sentences.

1 I drink coffee,   a but he doesn't study Spanish.

2 She plays football,   b but you love cats.

3 We don't live in London,   c but they don't like rock music.

4 David studies French,   d but she doesn't ski.

5 Kate and Sam like rap music,   e we live in Manchester.

6 You don't love dogs,   f but I don't drink tea.

Adverbs of frequency

⑤ Put the adverbs of frequency in the correct order along the line.

never   always   usually   often   sometimes

0%   100%

1 _never_   2 _____   3 _____   4 _____   5 _____

⑥ Put the words in the correct order.

1 have / we / at 7:30 / usually / breakfast

_____

2 me / sometimes / Dad / to school / drives

_____

3 is / late / Fiona / never

_____

4 always / they / cartoons / watch

_____

Need help? Go to page 54!

The present simple
(questions and short answers)

7 Complete the table.

question			short answer
Do	I		Yes, you do. / No, you don't.
¹ _____	you		Yes, I do. / No, I don't.
Does	he she it	play tennis?	Yes, he ² _____ . / No, he doesn't. Yes, she does. / No, she ³ _____ . Yes, it ⁴ _____ . / No, it ⁵ _____ .
⁶ _____	we you they		Yes, we do. / No, we don't. Yes, you ⁷ _____ . / No, you ⁸ _____ . Yes, they ⁹ _____ . / No, they ¹⁰ _____ .

8 Look at the pictures and write short answers.

1

Does Sally get up early?
No, she doesn't.

2

Does it rain here?
_____

3

Does she often go to
the cinema?
_____

4

Do they like rock
music?
_____

9 Write some things that you do at the weekend.

1 I always _____
2 I usually _____
3 I often _____
4 I sometimes _____
5 I never _____

Object pronouns

10 Complete the table.

subject	object
I	me
you	¹ _____
he	² _____
she	³ _____
it	⁴ _____
we	us
you	⁵ _____
they	⁶ _____

11 Complete the sentences with the correct pronoun.

1 Music and art are my favourite subjects.
   I like _____ a lot.
2 Her brother is horrible.
   I don't like _____ !
3 Miss Jones is our teacher.
   We all love _____ .
4 My aunt plays football. _____ is great!
5 Uncle David is a doctor. _____ works at
   the hospital.
6 Maths is very difficult. I don't like _____ .
7 We love our teachers and they love
   _____ .
8 Hello, how can I help _____ ?

Functions

Making suggestions

① **Listen and read.** 🔘⁸

Bill	That's the last piece of chocolate cake. Very nice.
Jane	What shall we do now?
Bill	Let's go to the cinema. There's a new *Space Wars* film on.
Jane	No, thanks! I don't really like that kind of film.
Ruth	Why don't we go to the art gallery?
Jane	Why? What's on there?
Ruth	There's an exhibition of photos of famous rock musicians.
Jane	That sounds good. What do you think, Bill?
Bill	I don't think so. It's not very exciting. Why don't we get the train to Wilkington?
Jane	But Wilkington's a small village. There's nothing there.
Bill	But today is different. There's a fair!
Ruth	Hey, that sounds really good!
Jane	OK, then. Let's walk down to the station and get the train to Wilkington.

② **Comprehension**

Read the conversation again. Tick (✓) the correct sentences.

1 a ◯ They all want to see Space Wars.

   b ◯ Only Bill wants to see Space Wars.

2 a ◯ The girls think the photo exhibition is a good idea.

   b ◯ Bill thinks the photo exhibition is a good idea.

3 a ◯ Wilkington is a big town.

   b ◯ Wilkington is a quiet place.

4 a ◯ They take the train to Wilkingon.

   b ◯ They walk to Wilkington.

③ **Reorder**

Put the words in the correct order to make sentences.

1 art / go / the / why / we / gallery / don't / to / ?
   Why don't we go to the Art Gallery?

2 station / down / let's / to / walk / the
   _____

3 visit / you / Venice / don't / why / ?
   _____

4 Wilkington / the / to / let's / fair / at / go /
   _____

④ **Read and write**

Write suggestions. Use *Let's …* and *Why don't we …* . Use the conversation above to help you.

1 There's an Air Show at Blackdean tomorrow.
   Let's go to the Air Show at
   Blackdean tomorrow.

2 There's a football match tonight.
   _____

3 There's a rock concert at your school on Friday night.
   _____

4 There's a party at David's house on Saturday.
   _____

5 There's a new film at the cinema.
   _____

⑤ **Write**

Imagine you are with your friends. Think about what's on in the next week or two. Write four suggestions for things you can do. Use *Let's …* and *Why don't we …*

1 _____

2 _____

3 _____

4 _____

Skills

① Listen

Listen to the family as they decide what to do at the weekend. Tick (✓) the correct sentences.

1. ◯ Mother wants to go to the fair.
2. ◯ Julie doesn't like fairs.
3. ◯ Mother says the fair is very boring.
4. ◯ Paul suggests the family goes to Bristol.
5. ◯ Paul says they can all go shopping in the morning.
6. ◯ Father wants to watch the football match.
7. ◯ Julie needs some new shoes.
8. ◯ Paul suggests they go to the cinema.

② Read

Read the text and answer the questions.

THE PAPERBOY

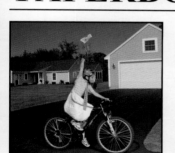

In Britain, people sometimes like to have a newspaper at home in the morning so that they can read it before they go to work. Many read their newspaper on the buses, too. Many teenagers deliver newspapers before they go to school in the mornings. Steve Brown is a paperboy in Blackdean. 'I get up at six o'clock every morning,' says Steve, 'and cycle to the paper shop.' Mr Roberts, the newsagent, gives me the papers. I put them into a big bag and cycle to the streets. I do about five streets. There are six of us who deliver newspapers. He pays us £15 each a week. I always finish by half past seven Then I go home to get ready for school.'

WORD LIST
teenager_____
cycle   _____
deliver   _____

1. Who delivers newspapers in Britain?
_____

2. What time does Steve get up in the morning?
_____

3. How many people deliver newspapers?
_____

4. How much money does Mr Roberts pay Steve?
_____

5. What does he do when he finishes work?
_____

③ Write

Write a paragraph about somebody you know who has a regular job. Use the following questions to help you.

✓ What time does he/she get up.
✓ What does he/she do in the mornings?
✓ What time does he/she have lunch?
✓ What does he/she do in the afternoons?
✓ What time does he/she finish?

Living in the Arctic!

① Read

Read the texts and complete the gaps with the words in the box.

> dinner   town   often   kilometres   doesn't work

○○○
◀ Back ▶ Forward ✕ Stop ⟳ Refresh 🏠 Home 🔍 Search
@ http://www.myfriends.com

About me

Tanya Anawak

- Age: 14
- Town: Iqaluit, Canada
- Languages: Inuktitut / English
- Brothers / Sisters: one brother, David
  one sister, Elisa
- I like: music / snowboarding
- I don't like: homework

My photos

This is my little sister, Elisa. She's so sweet!

This is my aunt and cousins. Fish for dinner tonight!

This is the outside of an igloo ....

... and this is the inside! It's quite warm!

Hi! My name's Tanya and I live in Iqaluit, a ¹ _____ in the north of Canada. It's in the Arctic and it's very cold!

I speak two languages. At home we speak Inuktitut and at school my lessons are in English.

My dad works in the local hospital but my mum ² _____ . She stays at home with my little sister, Elisa. She's only two years old. I've also got one brother, David. He's 11 years old.

People always ask me if we live in an igloo – the answer is no we don't! We live in a house about four ³ _____ from the centre of the town. After school I see my friends. There is a cool coffee shop in town where we ⁴ _____ go for a couple of hours.

For ⁵ _____ we usually eat meat or fish – but sometimes mum gives us a surprise, such as pizza and chips.

I love them!

Let's be friends!

Tanya

WORD LIST			
the Arctic	_____	inside	_____
coffee shop	_____	outside	_____
surprise	_____		

② Comprehension

Read the text again and answer the questions.

1 Where does Tanya live?
   She lives in Iqaluit in the north of Canada.

2 What languages does she speak?
   _____

3 Where does her dad work?
   _____

4 Do they live in an igloo?
   _____

5 What does she do after school?
   _____

6 What does she sometimes eat?
   _____

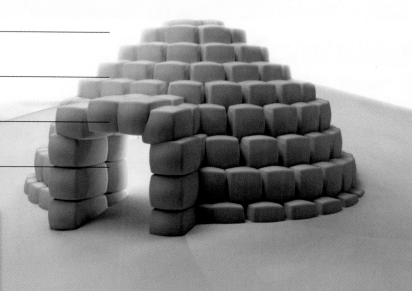

Igloos are small houses made of ice, but they can be warm and pleasant! If the external temperature outside is 40 degrees below zero, the temperature inside can be 16 degrees above zero!

CRACK THE CODE

③ **Complete the words and cross the letters off in the grid. A new word will appear.**

_f i s h_

__ __ z __ __ __

L	A	F	S	Z
P	C	H	G	O
S	I	U	U	I
S	Z	I	H	O
I	O	S	E	M

__ o __ __ __

m __ __ __ __

The new word is: _____

Free time

4

Vocabulary

① Match

Look at the pictures of the different activities. Match the people to the correct activities in the box.

> play rugby   dance   ski   do karate   skateboard   cook pasta   roller skate
>
> do gymnastics   dive   paint   play the piano   act

1 Paula: *dance*

4 Alice: _____

7 Susan: _____

10 Tim: _____

2 Chris: _____

5 Toby: _____

8 Mary: _____

11 Martin: _____

3 John: _____

6 Lisa: _____

9 Peter: _____

12 Sally: _____

② Choose

Look at the activities below. Tick (✓) the ones you can do, and cross (✗) the ones you can't do.

1 play basketball   ⬤

2 play the drums   ⬤

3 play the guitar   ⬤

4 do ballet   ⬤

5 speak English   ⬤

6 ice skate   ⬤

7 sing   ⬤

8 swim   ⬤

9 skateboard   ⬤

I can play the drums

③ Listen and read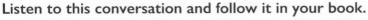

Listen to this conversation and follow it in your book.

Teacher	OK, listen everyone, please. I want to organise the end of year show. Tell me what you can do.
Harry	I can play the drums, Miss Clarke.
Tony	And I can play the piano.
Teacher	Good! Can anyone sing or play the guitar?
Beth	Yes, I can do both.
Teacher	Great! You can form a band for the show and play two or three songs! And you, Jill? What can you do?
Jill	Hmm … I can dance.
Teacher	Fantastic! Can you dance for us at the show?
Jill	OK. Miss Clarke, Kevin can dance too!
Teacher	Wow, can he? Excellent.
Kevin	No, I can't! Jill!
Teacher	Oh, OK. Now, Wendy, what can you do?
Wendy	I can do karate. I'm a black belt!
Teacher	Really? That's brilliant! Why don't you give a demonstration … with Kevin?
Wendy	Great! No problem.
Kevin	Oh, no!

④ Comprehension

Answer the questions.

1 What is the teacher's name?

_____

2 Who is in the band?

_____

3 Is Kevin a good dancer?

_____

4 Who is a black belt in karate?

_____

⑤ Find the words

Circle the 10 activities (across and down) in the word square.

D	A	N	C	E	Y	N	A	C	T
O	Y	U	O	O	F	D	E	O	L
J	E	S	T	S	K	I	D	O	J
U	T	F	I	Y	U	V	S	K	P
D	O	B	A	L	L	E	T	M	K
O	T	A	W	L	E	T	E	M	A
L	S	N	T	S	S	A	G	N	L
P	A	I	N	T	N	V	E	F	I
V	I	S	D	A	N	T	Y	J	E
P	L	A	Y	R	U	G	B	Y	B

Grammar

Can (ability)

① Complete the table.

affirmative			negative			question			short answer
I			I				I		Yes, I / you / he / she / it / we / you / they
You			You				you		
He			He				he		
She	can	sing.	She	¹ _____	sing.	² _____	she	sing?	³ _____ .
It			It				it		No, I / you / he / she / it / we / you / they
We			We				we		
You			You				you		
They			They				they		⁴ _____ .

② Look at the pictures and complete the sentences.

1  Jean _can ride a bike_ _____ .

2  Kate _____ .

3  Jim and Barbara _____ _____ .

4  Dad _____ .

5  Andy _____ .

6 My classmates _____ _____ .

③ Look at the sentences in Exercise 2 and make questions and short answers.

1 Jean: _____ Can Jean ride a bike? _____
   Yes, she can.

2 Kate: _____ ?
   Yes, she _____ .

3 Jim and Barbara: _____ ?
   No, they _____ .

4 Dad: _____ ?
   No, he _____ .

5 Andy: _____ ?
   Yes, _____ .

6 My classmates: _____ ?
   _____ .

Need help? Go to page 55!

The imperative

④ Complete the table.

affirmative	negative
Stand up.	Don't stand up.
Close your books.	1 _____
2 _____	Don't start.
Repeat.	3 _____

⑤ Match the phrases to the pictures.

Speak up.

Please sit down!

Don't shout!

Don't open the window!

1

_____
_____
_____

2

_____
_____
_____

3

_____
_____
_____

4

_____
_____
_____

Prepositions of place

⑥ Choose the correct preposition.

1

The mobile phone is
on / **in** the bag.

2

The apple is
on / **at** the table.

3

The map is
in / **on** the wall.

4

Alice is
under / **behind** the tree.

⑦ Look at the picture at the below. Complete the sentences using the prepositions in box.

behind	in front of
between	on next to

1 James is _____ the blackboard.
2 The blackboard is _____ the wall.
3 Mrs Williams is _____ the desk.
4 Helen is _____ the desk.
5 Monica is _____ Tom and Jane.

Functions

Asking for directions

① Listen and read. 🎧
Listen to the dialogue and
follow it in your books.

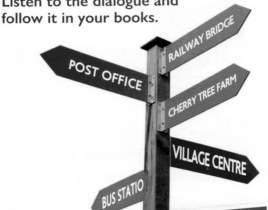

Steve	Well, I like this station, but how do we get to the farm?
Fiona	I don't know. Let's ask someone.
Sophia	Good idea! Look … there's a man over there.
Steve	Excuse me, can you tell us the way to the Cherry Tree farm, please?
Man	Oh, yes. Walk down this road into the village centre. Then turn left after the post office …
Sophia	And then?
Man	Then, go along the road and over the railway bridge. Go straight on and the farm is on the right, after the school.
Fiona	Thank you. Is it near?
Man	Oh yes, it's only about five kilometres.
Steve	Five kilometres?! Is there a bus?
Man	Yes … there are two each day!
Steve	Oh, no.
Sophia	Never mind. Let's walk!

WORD LIST
post office _____
railway bridge _____

---

② Comprehension
Read the questions and tick (✓) the correct answers.

1　a　They are at a shopping centre.　◯

　　b　They are at a train station.　◯

2　a　The man knows
　　　where the farm is.　◯

　　b　The man doesn't know
　　　where the farm is.　◯

3　a　The farm is on the left.　◯

　　b　The farm is on the right.　◯

4　a　They take the bus to the farm.　◯

　　b　They walk to the farm.　◯

③ Read
Read the dialogue again and look at the three maps below. Which one is the correct way to the fair?

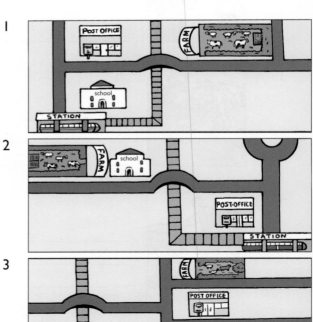

Skills

① Read

Read the text below.

What sport does Denise play?

Denise Parker can play tennis very well. She has lessons on Tuesdays and Thursdays and plays in the youth team for Blackdean Tennis Club. She often wins cups and medals in local competitions for the club. She is also the captain of the Queen Elizabeth School tennis team. She trains very hard in the gymnasium to keep fit, and she usually runs a few kilometres each week, too. She doesn't have time to play any other sports, although she always watches the football on television. Denise wants to become a professional tennis player when she leaves school and hopes to play at Wimbledon one day.

WORD LIST

train (v) _____
very hard _____

② Comprehension

Read the text again. Tick (✓) the correct sentences.

1 Denise is Captain of

   a   Blackdean Tennis Club. ◯

   b   her school tennis team. ◯

2 Denise has

   a   three tennis lessons each week. ◯

   b   two tennis lessons each week. ◯

3 Denise

   a   trains a lot. ◯

   b   doesn't train very much. ◯

① Listen

Listen to two people giving directions. Follow the directions on the map and circle the two destinations.

1

2

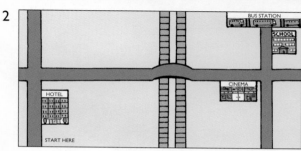

④ Write

Write directions for how to get somewhere you know, for example, from your home to school, from the station to the post office.

Dolphins

① Read

Read the texts and complete the gaps with the words in the box.

> teeth   intelligent   swim   minutes   metres

1   Dolphins can swim at 40 kilometres per hour!
2   Dolphins can hold their breath for ten ¹ _____ .
3   Dolphins live in big groups.
4   Dolphins live for about 25 years but some can live for 40 years!
5   Dolphins are very ² _____ and friendly animals. They are very curious and they like to play and have fun!
6   If there are dolphins in the sea, it means that the sea is clean. Dolphins don't like dirty water!
7   Dolphins sleep with one eye open and one eye closed. The open eye checks for danger when the dolphin is sleeping!
8   Dolphins sleep for eight hours a day and ³ _____ for 16 hours.
9   Some dolphins can jump five ⁴ _____ out of the water!
10 Dolphins have got lots of ⁵ _____ and they eat fish.

WORD LIST

hold their breath _____	mean (v) _____	open _____
curious _____	clean _____	danger _____
friendly _____	dirty _____	jump _____

② Comprehension

Decide which sentences are true (T) or false (F).
Correct the false sentences.

1 Dolphins can swim at 100 kilometres per hour.
_____

2 Dolphins usually live for about 25 years. _____
_____

3 Dolphins aren't very friendly. _____
_____

4 Dolphins eat fruit and vegetables.
_____

③ Write

Complete the sentences with *can*
or *can't* to make sentences about you.

1 I _____ swim.
2 I _____ hold my breath for ten minutes.
3 I _____ sleep with one eye open.
4 I _____ sleep for eight hours a day.

WOW!

Dolphins communicate
using their own language.
They even have names!

CRACK THE CODE

④ Look at the bubbles. Put the letters in the correct order to make a sentence.

1 _____   3 _____   5 _____
2 _____   4 _____   6 _____

① l s p o h d i h n

② t e a

③ i h s f

④ u b t

⑤ n o t

⑥ s h c p i

Descriptions

Vocabulary

① Complete

Look at the pictures and chose the words below which describe the people.

He / she is ...

~~plump~~   tall   average height

short   thin   slim

He / she has got ...

blue   long   wavy   short   dark

red   curly   blonde   ~~straight~~

brown   ~~medium length~~

Nick

Height: ¹ _____

Build: _____ *plump*

Hair: ² _____

³ _____

⁴ _____

Anna

Height: ⁵ _____

Build: ⁶ _____

Hair: ⁷ _____

⁸ _____

⁹ _____

Daniel

Height: ¹⁰ _____

Build: ¹¹ _____

Hair: *medium length*

¹² _____

straight

② Read

Read the description of Cristiano Ronaldo and circle the correct words.

Cristiano Ronaldo is ¹ **short /(tall)** and ² **slim / plump**. He's got short, ³ **dark / blonde** ⁴ **curly / straight** hair and ⁵ **blue / brown** eyes. He's a great footballer!

③ Write

Now describe yourself in the same way. Use the paragraph on Cristiano Ronaldo as a model.

1   I'm _____ .

2   I've got _____ .

Keith's new neighbour

④ Listen and read

Listen to the dialogue and follow it in your book.

Anna	Hey, who's that boy over there?
James	Which boy?
Anna	The one next to Mr Walters. He's got short dark hair and brown eyes.
James	Do you mean Robert?
Anna	No, Robert's average height and plump … this boy's really tall and slim.
James	Oh, OK, I can see him. That's Pal. He's from Poland. His parents now work in Blackdean. He's Keith's new neighbour. He's really good at football.
Anna	Cool. Let's go and meet him.
James	Hey, Pal. Come and meet Anna. Anna, this is Pal.
Pal	Hello, Anna. Nice to meet you.
Anna	Hi, Pal. Welcome to Blackdean. I hear you're a great footballer!
Pal	I'm OK at football, but my favourite sport is basketball, because I'm tall.
Anna	I like basketball too, but I'm not very good at it – I'm too short!

⑤ Comprehension

Read the dialogue again. Answer the questions below.

1 Who is the new boy at school?
   Pal is the new boy.

2 Is he tall?
   _____

3 Has Pal got blue eyes?
   _____

4 Who is plump?
   _____

5 What is Pal's favourite sport?
   _____

⑥ Find the sentence

There is one word in each line. Find the words to make a sentence.

P	A	L	I	E	N	W	G	J	K
T	Y	U	O	X	I	S	E	N	L
O	E	S	T	A	L	L	D	F	J
W	I	T	H	Y	U	I	T	O	K
X	Y	S	H	O	R	T	N	M	K
B	R	O	W	N	I	B	E	M	M
U	T	H	A	I	R	N	P	R	Y
P	U	A	N	D	W	A	G	N	M
T	I	N	H	S	B	R	O	W	N
E	Y	E	S	A	Y	T	Y	J	K

Write the sentence here:

_____

Grammar

Have got

① **Complete the table.**

affirmative	
I have got	I've got
you [1] _____ got	you've got
he has got	he [2] _____ got
she [3] _____ got	she [4] _____ got
it [5] _____	it [6] _____
we have got	we've got
you [7] _____ got	you [8] _____ got
they [9] _____	they [10] _____

negative	
I have not got	I haven't got
you [11] _____ got	you haven't got
he [12] _____ got	he has not got
she has not got	she [13] _____ got
it [14] _____ got	it [15] _____ got
we have not got	we [16] _____
you [17] _____ got	you haven't got
they have not got	they [18] _____

② **Look at the picture and complete the text.**

Dear Tom,

Here's a photo of my family. This is my mother. She [1] _____ long red hair and big blue eyes. This is my father. He [2] _____ short, grey hair and brown eyes. I [3] _____ twin brothers, their names are Rick and Ken. They [4] _____ short, brown, curly hair. We [5] _____ any pets.

③ **Complete the table.**

question			short answer
Have	I		Yes, you have. No, you haven't.
[1] _____	you		Yes, I [2] _____ . No, I haven't.
[3] _____	he		Yes, he has. No, he [4] _____ .
Has	she	got a sister?	Yes, she [5] _____ . No, she hasn't.
[6] _____	it		Yes, it has. No, it [7] _____ .
Have	we		Yes, we [8] _____ . No, we haven't.
[9] _____	you		Yes, you [10] _____ . No, you haven't.
[11] _____	they		Yes, they [12] _____ . No, they haven't.

④ **Look at the pictures and make questions and short answers using *have got*.**

1

she / red hair?
Has she got red hair?
No, she hasn't.

2

they / green car?
_____
_____

3

it / short legs?
_____
_____

4

he / a bike?
_____
_____

Need help? Go to page 56

Possessive 's

⑤ Look at the pictures and complete the labels.

1

Lisa's ___cat___

2

the children's _____

3

my parents' _____

⑥ Make sentences using the possessive 's.

1 My sister / camera phone

_____ is fantastic!

2 Our teacher / lessons

_____ are fun!

3 The boys / football

_____ is black and yellow.

4 Samantha and Jack / computer

_____ is new.

⑦ Put the words in the correct order to make sentences.

1 Vic / green / are / 's / eyes

_____

2 my grandparents / big / is / ' / very / house

_____

3 has got / Mike / 's / grey / father / hair

_____

4 hair / blonde / the girls / ' / is

_____

Possessive pronouns

⑧ Complete the table.

possessive adjectives	possessive pronouns
my	mine
your	1 _____
2 _____	his
her	3 _____
its	—
4 _____	ours
your	5 _____
6 _____	theirs

⑨ Look at the pictures and choose the correct words.

1

This isn't your ball.
It's **my** / **mine**.

2

This isn't my car.
It's **ours** / **his**.

3

That isn't my test.
It's **your** / **yours**.

4

This isn't your cake.
It's **theirs** / **mine**.

5

These aren't my clothes.
They're **his** / **hers**.

Functions

Buying a ticket

① Listen and read 🄬⁽¹⁴⁾

Amy	Thank you for carrying the teddy bear, Bob.
Bob	I hope your sister likes it. Look! Here's the bus.
Driver	Good afternoon. How can I help you?
Amy	Hello. Three tickets to Blackdean train station, please.
Driver	Single or return tickets?
Alison	Singles, please.
Driver	Are you students?
Amy	Bob isn't but Alison and I are students.
Driver	Have you got student cards?
Alison	Yes. I've got mine here. Have you got yours, Amy?
Amy	Oh, bother ... I haven't got mine with me.
Driver	Oh, no problem. So that's one full-price ticket and two student single tickets to Blackdean station ... and £5 for the teddy bear ... that's £9.75 please.
Bob	£5 for the teddy? No way!
Amy	Bob, calm down. It's a joke!

WORD LIST

single ticket	_____
return ticket	_____
teddy bear	_____

② Reorder

Put these dialogues in the correct order.

1
a   Are you a student? ⚪

b   That's £12.50 please. ⚪

c   How can I help you? ⚪

d   No I'm not. ⚪

e   Can I have a single to Bristol, please? ⚪

2
a   Here you are. ⚪

b   When do you want to travel? ⚪

c   That's £62.90, please. ⚪

d   On the four o'clock fast train. ⚪

e   Hello. We need three returns to London, please. ⚪

③ Write

You and a friend want to go to Bristol to see a rock concert. The concert starts at 19.30 and ends at 21.00. Look at the timetables on the left and decide which trains to catch. Then complete the conversation.

From Blackdean	To Bristol
14.20	15.30
15.30	17.00
17.10	18.20
18.10	19.30

From Bristol	To Blackdean
19.30	20.40
20.50	22.10
21.30	23.00
22.50	00.10

Clerk	Good afternoon. Can I help you?
You	Yes, please. ¹ _____ to Bristol, please.
Clerk	Is that two single tickets?
You	No, ² _____
Clerk	And what time do you want to come back?
You	³ _____
Clerk	OK. Are you students?
You	⁴ _____
Clerk	Right, that's £20.50, please.
You	⁵ _____
Clerk	Here are your tickets.
You	Thanks, goodbye.

① Listen and answer ⑮

Write the number of the person in the picture next to the names below.

1 Sammy ①   3 Carol ○

2 Mike ○   4 Lynn ○

② Write

Describe one of your friends. Write about the colour of his/her eyes and hair, how tall he/she is, what sort of person they are and what they like doing.

....
....
....
....
....
....
....
....
....

③ Read

Look at the picture above again. Complete the description.

That man over there [1] _____ the television, is James. He's a [2] _____ _____ of my brother's. He's very [3] _____ – nearly two metres – and he's got very [4] _____ blonde hair. His mother hates it! He's really nice. He [5] _____ in our basketball team – he's a great player. He's a student at the art college in Blackdean, and he's [6] _____ a friend called Milly – she's there [7] _____ the window. She's got [8] _____ dark hair and green eyes and she [9] _____ to be an actor when she leaves school.

Big cats

① Read

Read the texts and complete the gaps with the words in the box.

always	water	love	got

TIGERS

Tigers live in Asia. They are very strong animals and only eat meat. They have ¹ _____ orange and black stripes. All tigers are different – their stripes are never identical. Domestic cats don't like ² _____ but tigers can swim very well. They usually go swimming to cool off when they are too hot.

LEOPARDS

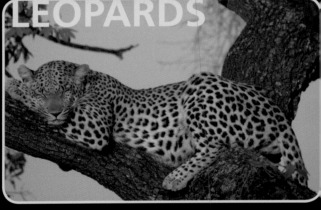

Leopards live in Africa and Asia. They also eat meat. All leopards have got black spots. They ³ _____ trees, because they really like to sleep there! They also look for food from trees. When they see an animal, first they jump on it, then they take it to the tree. They also like to fish!

LIONS

Lions live in Africa and Asia. They live in big groups. Sometimes there are 40 lions in one group. Male lions have got lots of hair and they protect the other lions in the group. Female lions look for food but the male lions ⁴ _____ eat first! Lions can eat 69 kilos of meat in one day!

WORD LIST

stripes	_____	spots	_____	protect	_____
domestic cats	_____	jump on	_____	female	_____
cool off	_____	male	_____		

② **Comprehension**

Read the text again. Look at the descriptions in the box and match them to the correct cat.

Tigers ...

_____

_____

_____

> live in big groups   have got stripes
>
> sleep in trees   have got lots of hair
>
> have got spots   can swim   are very strong
>
> can eat 69 kilos of meat   eat fish

Leopards ...

_____

_____

_____

All tigers are at risk of extinction. We must protect them if we do not want them to disappear from the planet.

Lions ...

_____

_____

_____

CRACK THE CODE

③ Use the code to find the letters and make words from the text. What's the new word?

A	D	E	F	G	I	L	M	N	O	P	R	S	T	U
15	14	13	12	11	10	9	8	7	6	5	4	3	2	1

9 **L**	10 **I**	6 **O**	7 **N**

2	4	13	13

11	4	6	1	5

3	5	6	2	3

8	13	15	2

3	2	4	10	5	13	3

12	6	6	14

Vocabulary

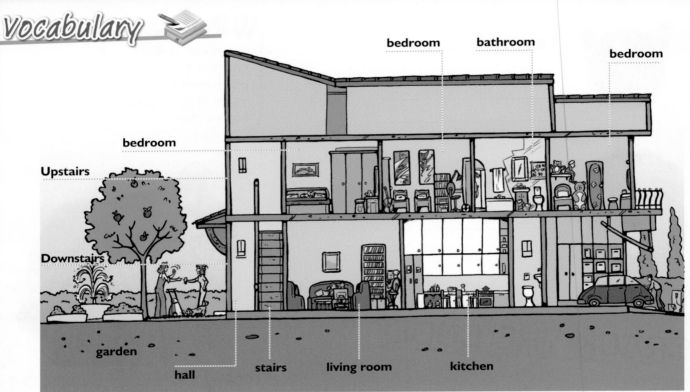

bedroom   bathroom

bedroom

bedroom

Upstairs

Downstairs

garden

hall   stairs   living room   kitchen

① Look and write

Look at the picture complete the table with the words in the box.
(Some things are in more than one place.)

bed   toilet   armchair   computer   table   sofa   bath   chair
television   cooker   wardrobe   tree   desk   mirror   picture
flowers   sink   cupboard   shower

kitchen	living room	bathroom	bedroom	garden
cooker				

What are you doing?

② Listen and read 🔘⁽¹⁶⁾

Listen to the dialogue and follow it in your book.

Tanya	Hello, Mrs Macintosh. Here's a cold drink … you look a bit hot. What are you doing?
Mum	Thanks, Tanya. Yes, I'm very busy today … I'm cleaning the kitchen, decorating the bathroom and also cutting the grass in the garden, and it's so hot!
Tanya	Wow, can I help?
Mum	That's very kind, thanks!
Tanya	No problem! Where's Mr Macintosh?
Mum	He's cleaning the car. What's Daniel doing? Is he doing his homework?
Tanya	Er … no, he isn't … he's playing a computer game in the living room.
Mum	What? He's relaxing in the living room. Daniel! Come out here.
Daniel	Hi, Mum. What are you both doing?
Mum	We're working! Come and help!
Daniel	Oh, no! I'm too tired!
Mum	Never mind! Cut the grass, please. We're going inside for a nice cold drink.
Daniel	Oh, no!

③ Comprehension

Read the dialogue again. Tick (✓) the correct sentences below.

1 Daniel is watching TV. ◯

2 Dad is cleaning the car. ◯

3 Mum is gardening. ◯

4 Joshua is playing a computer game. ◯

5 Tanya is helping Daniel's mum. ◯

6 Daniel is asking for a cold drink. ◯

④ Read and decide

Read the clues and decide which place or piece of furniture is being described.

1 Two or three people can sit on this.

    _s_ _o_ _f_ _a_

2 You put your clothes in this.

    w __ __ __ __ __ __ __

3 You can wash in this.

    __ a __ __

4 You keep food cold in this.

    __ __ __ __ g __

5 You cook food in this.

    __ o __ __ __ __

Grammar

The present continuous

① Complete the table.

affirmative		
full		contracted
I	am sleeping	'm sleeping
you	¹ _____	're sleeping
he	is sleeping	's sleeping
she	² _____	³ _____
it	⁴ _____	⁵ _____
we	⁶ _____	⁷ _____
you	⁸ _____	're sleeping
they	⁹ _____	¹⁰ _____

negative		
full		contracted
I	¹¹ _____	'm not sleeping
you	are not sleeping	¹² _____
he	¹³ _____	isn't sleeping
she	¹⁴ _____	¹⁵ _____
it	is not sleeping	¹⁶ _____
we	¹⁷ _____	¹⁸ _____
you	¹⁹ _____	aren't sleeping
they	are not sleeping	²⁰ _____

② Make these positive sentences negative.

1 I Daniel is watching TV.
Daniel isn't watching TV.

2 Joshua and Lizzie are playing in the bedroom.
_____

3 Mrs Robinson is sunbathing in the garden.
_____

4 I am drinking a coffee.
_____

5 You are studying for a French exam.
_____

6 We are writing a story.
_____

③ Complete the table.

question			short answer
Am	I		Yes, you are. No, you aren't.
¹ _____	you		Yes, I am. No, I ² _____
Is	he		Yes, he ³ _____ No, he ⁴ _____
⁵ _____	she	sleeping?	Yes, she is. No, she ⁶ _____
⁷ _____	it		Yes, it ⁸ _____ No, it ⁹ _____
Are	we		Yes, we ¹⁰ _____ No, we aren't.
¹¹ _____	you		Yes, you are. No, you ¹² _____
Are	they		Yes, they ¹³ _____ No, they ¹⁴ _____

④ Look at the pictures. Answer the questions about what these people are doing.

1   Is Philip washing the car?
No he isn't.
He's listening to music.

2 Are the dogs playing with the ball?
_____
_____

3 Is Susan singing?
_____
_____

4  Is David cutting the grass?
_____
_____

Need help? Go to page 57!

Johnny

Frank

Paul

You

Mum

Dad

Jackie

Louise

Megan

⑤ **Write questions and short answers.**

1   Johnny / dive?
    Is Johnny diving?
    Yes he is.

2   Paul / swim / in the pool?
    _____
    _____

3   Dad / speak / to Mum?
    _____
    _____

4   you / buy / ice cream?
    _____
    _____

5   Mum / read / a newspaper?
    _____
    _____

6   Jackie / wear / sunglasses?
    _____
    _____

⑥ **Complete the conversation. Use the correct form of the verbs.**

Jackie: Hey Megan, what
1 *are you doing?* (do)?

Megan: Sssh, I 2 _____ (try) to
write a letter!

Jackie: Who 3 _____ (write) to?

Megan: That's a secret!

Louise: Oh, come on, tell us!
4 _____ (write) a love
letter?

Megan: No, I 5 _____ (not be)!
Hey Jackie, where's your brother
Frank?

Jackie: He's in the pool with Paul.
They 6 _____ (have)
a swimming competition!

Megan: Who 7 _____ (win)?
Frank?

Louise: No, he 8 _____ (not be).
I think it's Paul. He's strong!

Megan: Oh, that's a shame.

Louise: I know who 9 _____ (write)
to. It's Frank!

Jackie: Yes, it's a letter to my brother!

Functions

Talking about likes and dislikes

① Listen and read

Listen to the dialogue and follow it in your book.

Woman	Excuse me, could I ask you some questions for a survey about what sports teenagers like and don't like?
Joanne	Yes, sure.
Woman	So, what's your favourite sport?
Deborah	Well, I really like volleyball but I love tennis. I'm a member of the local club.
James	She doesn't love tennis – she loves the club!
Joanne	Be quiet! I like volleyball too, but I prefer gymnastics. I also quite like badminton.
James	I hate badminton!
Joanne	Shut up! You're not a teenager!
Woman	OK, and what sports don't you like?
Deborah	I don't like rugby. I think it's very boring!
Woman	What about you?
Joanne	Well, I quite like rugby but I hate football.

② Comprehension

Match the words to make true sentences about the dialogue above.

1 Deborah loves
2 Joanne likes
3 James hates
4 Deborah doesn't like
5 Joanne hates

a volleyball.
b rugby.
c football.
d tennis.
e badminton.

③ Reorder

Put these verbs in order from hate (1) to love (6).

> hate   love   really like
> don't like   like   quite like

1 *hate*   2 _____   3 _____   4 _____   5 _____   6 *love*

④ Write

Look at the pictures. Then write sentences that are true for you.

1

I love pizza.
_____

2

_____
_____

3

_____
_____

4

_____
_____

Skills

① Listen and answer 🔘⑱

Listen to the people and put a tick (✓) under what they like and a cross (X) under what they don't like.

	football	tennis	horse riding	skiing	gymnastics	computer games
Bob						
Lynn						
Andy						
Clare						

② Read

Read the text. How many musical instruments does Flora play?

Flora Brett is 14 years old and lives in Canterbury with her mum and her older brother, Felix. She's a very musical girl! She can play many musical instruments and also sings very well. She quite likes the saxophone and the guitar but the piano is her favourite. Now she is learning the drums, too! Flora practises her music three hours every day, so she is very busy.

When she's got time, she goes to the cinema with her friends. They don't like violent films. They prefer musical films with Zac Efron!

Flora is also a good actress and she's a member of a local drama club. She doesn't like swimming very much and she really hates shopping. She loves animals and she has got a cat, two dogs and a goldfish.

③ Comprehension

Answer the questions.

1. 1 Who does Flora live with?

   _____

2. What is Flora's favourite musical instrument?

   _____

3. How many hours a day does she practise?

   _____

4. What activities doesn't she like?

   _____

④ Write

Write a profile of someone you know well. Use the profile of Flora Brett to help you. Remember to include:

✓ Their name

✓ Their age

✓ Where they live

✓ What they like

✓ What they don't like

Elephants

① Read the text. What do we call a group of elephants?

Elephants have fantastic memories!
They remember other elephants and they also often remember places where they go to eat and drink.

Elephants eat for 16 hours a day!
Elephants don't eat meat but they eat lots and lots of plants, fruits and leaves. When they aren't eating they drink, wash, play, rest and sleep.

Elephants can't jump!
They have got 4 knees but they can't jump. They can run at 40 kilometres per hour!

Elephants live in small families!
Elephants are very friendly animals. They live in small families led by the oldest female elephant of the group. When many families live together we call it a 'herd'.

WORD LIST

memories	_____	rest	_____	jump	_____
remember	_____	knees	_____	led by	_____

50

② **Comprehension**

Read the text about elephants again. Are the sentences true (T) or false (F)?

1 Elephants never remember places or other elephants. ◯

2 Elephants eat for five hours a day. ◯

3 Elephants don't eat meat. ◯

4 Elephants can jump very high. ◯

The ears of the African elephant are very important. They wave them to cool down when they are hot and they open them wide to show danger or anger.

③ **Write**

Match the verbs in the box to the pictures.
Then write the correct form of the present continuous.

drink   walk   play   eat

1 they _____   2 he _____   3 he _____   4 they _____

CRACK THE CODE

④ **Look at the two elephant footprints. Which of the five words is the odd one out? Write the words in the two spaces.**

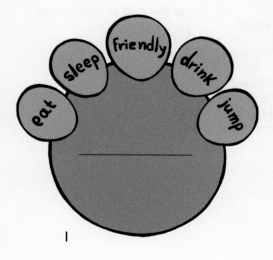

eat   sleep   friendly   drink   jump

_____

1

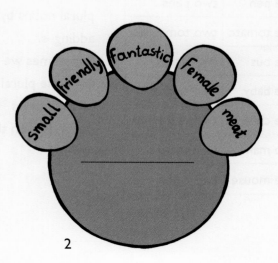

small   friendly   fantastic   female   meat

_____

2

Grammar reference

Grammar Unit 1

① Personal pronouns (subject)

I
you
he
she
it
we
you
they

▶ We use subject personal pronouns to show who or what does something.

② Possessive adjectives

my
your
his
her
its
our
your
their

▶ We use possessive adjectives before a noun to say who or what something belongs to, or is related to.

③ The verb be (present simple)

affirmative		negative		question	short answer
full	contracted	full	contracted		
I am	I'm	I am not	I'm not	Am I?	Yes, you are. / No, you aren't.
you are	you're	you are not	you aren't	Are you?	Yes, I am. / No, I'm not.
he is	he's	he is not	he isn't	Is he?	Yes, he is. / No, he isn't.
she is	she's	she is not	she isn't	Is she?	Yes, she is. / No, she isn't.
it is	it's	it is not	it isn't	Is it?	Yes, it is. / No, it isn't.
we are	we're	we are not	we aren't	Are we?	Yes, we are. / No, we aren't.
you are	you're	you are not	you aren't	Are you?	Yes, you are. / No, you aren't.
they are	they're	they are not	they aren't	Are they?	Yes, they are. / No, they aren't.

▶ The contracted form is informal in spoken and written English. The full form is formal.

④ Plurals

one pen	two pens
one tomato	two tomatoes
one bus	two buses
one baby	two babies
one child	two children
one man	two men
one mouse	two mice

▶ We form most plural nouns by adding -s.

▶ Sometimes we form the plural noun with -es depending on the ending.

⑤ Question words

What?
Who?
Where?
When?
How?

▶ We place a question mark (?) at the end of a question.

Grammar Unit 2

① *There is / There are*

	affirmative	negative	question	short answer
singular	there is (there's)	there is not (there isn't)	Is there …?	Yes, there is. / No, there isn't.
plural	there are	there are not (there aren't)	Are there …?	Yes, there are. / No, there aren't.

▶ We use *There is* (singular) and *There are* (plural) to describe what is in a place.

▶ *There is* can be shortened to *There's*. *There are* can not be shortened.

② *a / an*

▶ We use *a* before a word with a consonant sound:

a pen   a school   a dog

▶ We use *an* before a word with a vowel sound:

an apple   an orange   an elephant   an hour

③ Countable and uncountable nouns

▶ *Books, pens, houses* are countable because they describe amounts that can we can count.

▶ *Rice, water, coffee* are uncountable because they describe amounts that we can not count.

④ *some / any*

	affirmative	negative	question
uncountable nouns	There is **some** cheese.	There isn't **any** salt.	Is there **any** tea?
plural countable nouns	There are **some** bananas.	There aren't **any** cakes.	Are there **any** apples?

▶ *Some* and *any* describe indefinite amounts.

▶ We use them with with uncountable nouns and plural countable nouns.

▶ We use *some* in affirmative sentences and we use *any* in negative sentences and questions.

⑤ *How much / How many*

▶ We use *How much* with uncountable nouns. *How much sugar?*

▶ We use *How many* with countable plural nouns. *How many boys?*

Grammar reference

Grammar Unit 3

① The present simple

affirmative	negative	question	short answer
I work	I do not (don't) work	Do I work?	Yes, you do. / No, you don't.
you work	you do not (don't) work	Do you work?	Yes, I do. / No, I don't.
he works	he does not (doesn't) work	Does he work?	Yes, he does. / No, he doesn't.
she works	she does not (doesn't) work	Does she work?	Yes, she does. / No, she doesn't.
it works	it does not (doesn't) work	Does it work?	Yes, it does. / No, it doesn't.
we work	we do not (don't) work	Do we work?	Yes, we do. / No, we don't.
you work	you do not (don't) work	Do you work?	Yes, you do. / No, you don't.
they work	they do not (don't) work	Do they work?	Yes, they do. / No, they don't.

▶ We use the present simple to describe habits or recurring actions.
   I go to school every day.   **I sometimes go jogging in the morning.**
▶ We add -s to the third person singular.
▶ We add -es when the verb ends in -o, -ss, -tch, -x or -y (when preceded by a consonant).
   go → go**es**
   kiss → kiss**es**
   wash → wash**es**
   watch → watch**es**
   mix → mix**es**
   fly → fl**ies**
   N.B. play → play**s**
   We use the auxiliary do/don't or does/doesn't in questions, negative sentences and short answers.

② Adverbs of frequency

always	usually	often	sometimes	never
100%				0%

▶ We use adverbs of frequency with the present simple to indicate how often something happens.
▶ They go before the verb (I **never play** football.), but after the verb be and modal verbs (She**'s always** angry.)

③ Object pronouns

me
you
him, her, it
us
you
them

▶ We use object pronouns instead of a noun
   that has been expressed.
   I have a sister.   I love her. (= my sister)
▶ They go after a verb or preposition.
   I love her. Look at me.

Grammar Unit 4

① Can (ability)

affirmative	negative	question	short answer
I can	I cannot (can't)	Can I?	Yes, you can. / No, you can't.
you can	you cannot (can't)	Can you?	Yes, I can. / No, I can't.
he can	he cannot (can't)	Can he?	Yes, he can. / No, he can't.
she can	she cannot (can't)	Can she?	Yes, she can. / No, she can't.
it can	it cannot (can't)	Can it?	Yes, it can. / No, it can't.
we can	we cannot (can't)	Can we?	Yes, we can. / No, we can't.
you can	you cannot (can't)	Can you?	Yes, you can. / No, you can't.
they can	they cannot (can't)	Can they?	Yes, they can. / No, they can't.

- ▶ *Can* has the same form for all subjects (*I, you, he*, etc.)
- ▶ The main verb after *can* is the infinitive without *to*.
- ▶ We use *can* to express ability:

   She can speak French.

② The imperative

affirmative	negative
Speak up!	Don't move!
Open the door!	Don't touch it!

- ▶ To form of imperative we use the infinitive of the verb without *to* (the bare infinitive).
- ▶ We do not express the subject. We understand that the subject is *you*.
- ▶ To form the negative we use *don't*.

③ Prepositions of place

prepositions of place	
in	The book is **in** the bag.
on	The cat is **on** the car.
under	The ball is **under** the table.
behind	The boy is **behind** the tree.
in front of	The man is **in front of** the house.
between	The cinema is **between** the station and the hotel.
next to	The cheese is **next to** the butter.

Grammar reference

Grammar Unit 5

① *Have got*

affirmative		negative	
full	**contracted**	**full**	**contracted**
I have got	I've got	I have not got	I haven't got
you have got	you've got	you have not got	you haven't got
he has got	he's got	he has not got	he hasn't got
she has got	she's got	she has not got	she hasn't got
it has got	it's got	it has not got	it hasn't got
we have got	we've got	we have not got	we haven't got
you have got	you've got	you have not got	you haven't got
they have got	they've got	they have not got	they haven't got

question	short answer	
Have I got?	Yes, you have. / No you haven't.	
Have you got?	Yes, I have. / No I haven't.	
Has he got?	Yes, he has. / No he hasn't.	
Has she got?	Yes, she has. / No she hasn't.	
Has it got?	Yes, it has. / No it hasn't.	
Have we got?	Yes, we have. / No we haven't.	
Have you got?	Yes, you have. / No you haven't.	
Have they got?	Yes, they have. / No they haven't.	

▶ We use the verb *have got* to show possession.

I've got a skateboard.

Have you got a pet?

I haven't got a bike.

▶ We don't use *got* in short answers.

▶ We don't use *got* in the expressions.

have breakfast / lunch / dinner / a shower

② Possessive *'s*

singular	irregular plurals
the girl**'s** bedroom	the children**'s** bedroom
plural	**two subjects**
the girls**'** bedroom	Rachel and Anna**'s** bedroom

▶ We use the possessive 's to show possession

▶ We use the possessive 's after a person's name, even if it ends in -s.

▶ We use the possessive 's after a singular noun.

▶ When the noun is plural, the apostrophe goes after the s.

③ Possessive pronouns

possessive adjectives	possessive pronouns
my	mine
your	yours
his	his
her	hers
its	–
our	ours
your	yours
their	theirs

▶ There is no possessive pronoun of *its*.

Grammar Unit 6

① The present continuous

affirmative		negative	
full	**contracted**	**full**	**contracted**
I am walking	I'm walking	I am not walking	I'm not walking
you are walking	you're walking	you are not walking	you aren't walking
he is walking	he's walking	he is not walking	he isn't walking
she is walking	she's walking	she is not walking	she isn't walking
it is walking	it's walking	it is not walking	it isn't walking
we are walking	we're walking	we are not walking	we aren't walking
you are walking	you're walking	you are not walking	you aren't walking
they are walking	they're walking	they are not walking	they aren't walking

question	short answer
Am I walking?	Yes, you are. / No, you aren't.
Are you walking?	Yes, I am. / No, I'm not.
Is he walking?	Yes, he is. / No, he isn't.
Is she walking?	Yes, she is. / No, she isn't.
Is it walking?	Yes, it is. / No, it isn't.
Are we walking?	Yes, we are. / No, we aren't.
Are you walking?	Yes, you are. / No, you aren't.
Are they walking?	Yes, they are. / No, they aren't.

▸ We use the present continuous to describe an action that is happening at or around the moment of speaking.

▸ We form the present continuous with the verb *be* and the main verb with -*ing* (the present participle).

▸ We don't use the present participle in short answers.

- With verbs that end in a consonant + -e, we change the -e to -*ing*.

  chase → chas**ing**   dance → danc**ing**

- With most verbs that end in a single vowel + a consonant, we double the consonant and add -*ing*.

  win → win**ning**   get → get**ting**

- With verbs that end in -*ie*, we change the -*ie* to -ying.

  lie → l**ying**   die → d**ying**

Word list

Unit 1

always /ˈɔːlweɪz/

aunt /ɑːnt/ /

beautiful /ˈbjuːtɪfʊl/

best friend /ˈbest ˌfrend/

big /bɪg/

birthday party /ˈbɜːθdeɪ ˈpɑːti/

Britain /ˈbrɪtən/

brother /ˈbrʌðə/

cat /kæt/

child, children /tʃaɪld, ˈtʃɪldrən/

Christmas Day /ˈkrɪsməs deɪ/

classmate /ˈklɑːsmeɪt/

close (v) /kləʊz/

clothes /kləʊðz/

cold /kəʊd/

cool place /kuːl pleɪs/

country /ˈkʌntri/

cousin /ˈkʌzən/

doctor /ˈdɒktə/

dog /dɒg/

Easter /ˈiːstə/

England /ˈɪŋglənd/

English /ˈɪŋglɪʃ/

everybody /ˈevribɒdi/

exotic /ɪgˈzɒtɪk/

father /ˈfɑːðə/

festival /ˈfestɪvəl/

flower /flaʊə/

girlfriend /ˈgɜːlfrend/

grandfather /ˈgrændfɑːðə/

grandmother /ˈgrændmʌðə/

grandparents /ˈgrænpeərənts/

happy /ˈhæpi/

high /haɪ/

holiday /ˈhɒlɪdeɪ/

hot /hɒt/

hospital /ˈɒspɪtəl/

house /haʊs/

hungry /ˈhʌŋgri/

life /laɪf/

like (v) /laːk/

little /ˈlɪtəl/

long /lɒŋ/

lovely /ˈlʌvli/

May Day /ˈmeɪ ˌdeɪ/

mother /ˈmʌðə/

new /njuː/

New Year's Day /njuː jiəz deɪ/

nice /naɪs/

on the right /ɒn ðə raɪt/

other /ˈʌðə/

outside /ˌaʊtˈsaɪd/

parents /ˈpeərənts/

people /ˈpiːpəl/

play (v) /pleɪ/

Poland /ˈpəʊlənd/

rain (n) /reɪn/

sad /sæd/

season /ˈsiːzən/

sister /ˈsɪstə/

small /smɔːl/

snow (v) /snəʊ/

snow (n) /snəʊ/

south /saʊθ/

Spain /speɪn/

spring /sprɪŋ/

summer /ˈsʌmə/

sun /sʌn/

sunny /ˈsʌni/

surname /ˈsɜːneɪm/

thirsty /ˈθɜːsti/

uncle /ˈʌŋkəl/

Valentine's Day /ˈvæləntaɪnz deɪ/

wear (v) /weə/

weather /ˈweðə/

west /west/

wind /wɪnd/

winter /ˈwɪntə/

young /jʌŋ/

Unit 2

altogether /ˌɑːltəˈgeðə/

apple /ˈæpəl/

banana /bəˈnɑːnə/

beans /biːnz/

beer /bɪə/

biscuit /ˈbɪskɪt/

box /bɒx/

bottle /ˈbɒtəl/

bread /bred/

breakfast /ˈbrekfəst/

butter /ˈbʌtə/

cake /keɪk/

certainly /ˈsɜːtənli/

cheese /tʃiːz/

chicken /ˈtʃɪkɪn/

chips /tʃɪps/

chocolate /ˈtʃɒklɪt/

cup /kʌp/

dairy /ˈdeəri/

dinner /ˈdɪnə/

drink /drɪŋk/

egg /eg/

fish /fɪʃ/

fridge /frɪdʒ/

fruit /fruːt/

half /hɑːf/

ice cream /ˈaɪsˌkriːm/

iced tea /ˌaɪst ˈtiː/

large /lɑːdʒ/

lamb /læm/

lunch /lʌntʃ/

meat /miːt/

milk /mɪlk/

orange /ˈɒrɪndʒ/

orange juice /ˈɒrɪndʒ dʒuːs/

pear /peə/

pie /paɪ/

pineapple /ˈpaɪnæpəl/

pint /paɪnt/

potato /pəˈteɪtəʊ/

rice /raɪs

salt /sɒlt/

sandwich /ˈsæwɪdʒ/

smoothie /ˈsmuːði/

sugar /ˈʃʊgə/

tomato /təˈmɑːtəʊ/

truth /truːθ/

tuna /ˈtjuːnə/

vegetable /ˈvedʒtəbəl/

wait (v) /weɪt/

water /ˈwɒtə/

Unit 3

art gallery /ɑːt ˈgæləri/

at home /æt həʊm/

bicycle /ˈbaɪsɪkəl/

bus /bʌs/

busy /ˈbɪzi/

computer game /kəmˈpjuːtə geɪm/

difficult /ˈdɪfɪkəlt/

drive (v) /draɪv/

each /iːtʃ/

early /ˈɜːli/

eat (v) /iːt/

exciting /ɪkˈsaɪtɪŋ/

exhibition /ˌeksɪˈbɪʃən/

football /ˈfʊtbɔːl/

French /frentʃ/

get ready for (v) /get redi fɔː/

get up (v) /get ʌp/

give (v) /gɪv/

have a shower (v) /hæv ə ʃaʊə/

homework /ˈhəʊmwɜːk/

kind /kaɪnd/

late /leɪt/

learn (v) /lɜːn/

leave (v) /liːv/

love (v) /lʌv/

match /mætʃ/

maths /mæθs/

meat (n) /miːt/

Word list

meet (v) /miːt/

money /ˈmʌni/

near /nɪə/

need (v) /niːd/

never /ˈnevə/

newsagent /ˈnjuːzeɪdʒənt/

night /naɪt/

nothing /ˈnʌθɪŋ/

often /ˈafən/

paper shop /ˈeɪpə ʃap/

pay (v) /peɪ/

piece /piːs/

quiet /ˈkwaɪət/

ski /skiː/

sometimes /ˈsʌmtaɪmz/

Spanish /ˈspænɪʃ/

station /ˈsteɪʃən/

street /striːt/

suggest (v) /səˈdʒest/

take (v) /teɪk/

tomorrow /təˈmarəʊ/

tonight /təˈnaɪt/

town /taʊn/

train /treɪn/

usually /ˈjuːʒʊəli/

village /ˈvɪlɪdʒ/

wash (v) /waʃ/

washing up /ˈwaʃɪŋ ʌp/

watch TV /watʃɪŋ ˌtiːˈviː/

work (v) /wɜːk/

Unit 4
act (v) /ækt/

ballet /ˈbæleɪ/

basketball /ˈbaːskɪtbɔːl/

blackboard /ˈblækbɔːd/

black belt /ˈblæk ˌbelt/

both /bəʊθ/

captain /ˈkæptɪn/

church /tʃɜː/

competition /ˌkampɪˈtɪʃən/

cook pasta /kʊk ˈpæstə/

cup /kʌp/

dance (v) /daːns/

demonstration /ˌdemənˈstreɪʃən/

dive (v) /daɪv/

drums /drʌmz/

end of year show / end əv jiə ʃəʊ/

excuse me /ɪkˈskjuːz mi/

farm /faːm/

form (v) /fɔːm/

go straight on /gəʊ streɪt an/

gymnastics /dʒɪmˈnæstɪks/

ice skate (v) /ˈaɪs ˌskeɪt/

keep fit (v) /ˌkiːp ˈfɪt/

lesson /ˈlesən/

medal /ˈmedəl/

paint (v) /peɪnt/

play the piano /pleɪ ðə piˈænəʊ/

ride a bike /raɪd ə baɪk/

roller skate (v) /ˈrəʊlə ˌskeɪt/

rucksack /ˈrʌksæk/

sail (v) /seɪl/

sing (v) /sɪŋ/

someone /ˈsʌmwʌn/

swim (v) /swɪm/

tennis player /ˈtenɪs ˈpleɪjə/

tree /triː/

turn (v) /tɜːn/

wall /wɔːl/

Unit 5
actor /ˈæktə/

average height /ˈævərɪdʒ haɪt/

blonde /bland/

blue /bluː/

brown /braʊn/

cheap /tʃiːp/

curly /ˈkɜːli/

dark /daːk/

fun /fʌn/

Word list

garden /'gɑːdən/

good at /gʊd æt/

good-looking /ˌgʊd 'lʊkɪŋ/

green /griːn/

grey /greɪ/

horse /hɔːs/

joke /dʒəʊk/

leg /leg/

long /laŋ/

medium length /'miːdiəm leŋθ/

neighbour /'neɪbə/

plump /plʌmp/

pretty /'prɪti/

red /red/

short /ʃɔːt/

slim /slɪm/

straight /streɪt/

student card /'stjuːdənt kɑːd/

tall /tɔːl/

teddy bear /'tedi beə/

thin /θɪn/

together /tə'geðə/

wavy /'weɪvi/

window /'wɪndəʊ/

Unit 6
armchair /'ɑːmtʃeə/

bath /bɑːθ/

bathroom /'bɑːθruːm/

bed /bed/

bedroom /'bedruːm/

chair /tʃeə/

clean (v) /kliːn/

cooker /'kʊkə/

cupboard /'kʌbəd/

cut (v) /kʌt/

decorate (v) /'dekəreɪ/

desk /desk/

drama club /'drɑːmə klʌb/

garden (v) /'gɑːdən/

grass /grɑːs/

hall /hɔːl/

hate (v) /heɪt/

horse riding /hɔːs 'raɪdɪŋ/

inside /ˌɪn'saɪd/

kitchen /'kɪtʃɪn/

living room /'lɪvɪŋ ruːm/

mirror /'mɪrə/

musical instrument /'mjuːzɪkəl 'ɪnstəmənt/

picture /'pɪktʃə/

pool /puːl/

relax (v) /rɪ'læks/

saxophone /'sæksəfəʊn/

sink /sɪŋk/

sofa /'səʊfə/

stairs /stæz/

sunbathe (v) /'sʌnbeɪð/

sunglasses /'sʌnglɑːsɪz/

survey /'sɜːveɪ/

table /'teɪbəl/

toilet /'tɔɪlət/

volleyball /'valibɔːl/

wardrobe /'wɔːdrəʊb/

Exit test

Name _____ Surname _____ Class _____ Date _____

① Complete the sentences with the correct object pronouns.

e.g. *There's a dog in the street. I'm watching ___it___ .*

1 Jane's a nice girl. I like _____ .

2 My family's going to the cinema. Paul's coming with _____ .

3 I'm speaking to Sue, and she's speaking to _____ .

4 My grandparents live in Spain. I don't live with _____ .

② Complete the sentences with the correct possessive adjectives.

e.g. *Danny is visiting ___his___ grandparents.*

1 Lucy is doing _____ homework.

2 We often work in _____ garden.

3 The boys love _____ bikes.

4 The dog is playing with _____ ball.

5 I love _____ new bag. Thanks, Mum!

③ Complete the sentences with some or any.

e.g. *There are ___some___ biscuits on the table.*

1 There isn't _____ milk in the fridge.

2 There's _____ bread in the cupboard.

3 Is there _____ money in your bag?

4 There are _____ books on the table.

5 Are there _____ chairs in the kitchen?

④ Are these nouns countable (C) or uncountable (U)?

e.g. *apple ___C___*

1	cat	_____	5	book	_____
2	rice	_____	6	party	_____
3	water	_____	7	banana	_____
4	coffee	_____	8	milk	_____

⑤ Complete the sentences with the correct form of the present simple.

e.g. *(work) I ___work___ in a bank.*

1 (live) She _____ in Manchester.

2 (play) _____ you _____ football?

3 (not like) He _____ pop music.

4 (go) Wher e_____ she _____ on holiday?

⑥ Put a line (/) where the adverb of frequency goes in these sentences.

e.g. *(usually) I / go to work by bus.*

1 (never) She comes to school on time.

2 (often) Does he go and visit them?

3 (always) Do you wear a hat in the summer?

4 (usually) We eat at the Indian restaurant.

⑦ **Correct these sentences with** *can*.

e.g. *Peter cans speak German.*
   Peter can speak German.

1 I canot go to school tomorrow.

2 He can to swim very well.

3 You can ride a bike?

4 Can she play the piano?
   Yes, she does.

⑧ **Put the words in the correct order to make sentences.**

e.g. *new / is / ' / green / my / s / brother / car*
   My brother's new car is green.

1 computer / s / doesn't / David / ' / work

2 big / the / house / is / ' / Browns / very

3 often / ' / women / team / the / football / s / wins

4 s / Chip / our / ' / name / dog / is

⑨ **Write the correct question word.**

e.g. *What is that in your hand?*
   It's my pet mouse.

1 _____ is that boy over there?
   It's Pal, the new boy from Poland.

2 _____ is my school bag?
   It's next to the door.

3 _____ are you?
   Very well, thanks.

4 _____ time does the football match start?
   At half-past two.

⑩ **Complete the sentences with the correct form of** *have got*.

e.g. *The Browns have got have got a new car.*

1 _____ you _____ a pen?
2 Janet _____ not _____ any books.
3 _____ he _____ a bike?
4 They _____ not _____ any children.

⑪ **Complete the sentences with the correct form of the present continuous.**

e.g. *It is raining today. (rain)*

1 Peter _____ now. (not work)
2 _____ they _____ a British film? (watch)
3 Liz _____ her grandparents today. (visit)
4 _____ Dan _____ computer games in his room? (play)

Total: _____ / 46

HEINLE
CENGAGE Learning™

Holiday Explorer 1
David A. Hill

Publisher: Jason Mann

Adaptations Manager: Alistair Baxter

Assistant Editor: Manuela Barros

Senior Marketing Manager: Ruth McAleavey

Senior Content Project Editor: Natalie Griffith

Senior Production Controller: Paul Herbert

National Geographic Liaison: Leila Hishmeh

Art Director: Natasa Arsenidou

Cover Designer: Nora Spiliopoulou

Text Designer: Alexandra Bacoyianni

Audio: EFS Television Production Ltd

Acknowledgements

The publisher gratefully acknowledges the editorial contribution of Lisa Darrand.

The publisher would also like to thank Bethan Williams for her invaluable contribution.

© 2011 Heinle, Cengage Learning

ALL RIGHTS RESERVED. No part of this work covered by the copyright herein may be reproduced, transmitted, stored or used in any form or by any means graphic, electronic or mechanical, including but not limited to photocopying, recording, scanning, digitising, taping, Web distribution, information networks, or information storage and retrieval systems, except as permitted under Section 107 or 108 of the 1976 United States Copyright Act, without the prior written permission of the publisher.

For permission to use material from this text or product, submit all requests online at **cengage.com/permissions** Further permissions questions can be emailed to **permissionrequest@cengage.com**

ISBN: 978-1-111-40059-0

Heinle, Cengage Learning EMEA
Cheriton House
North Way
Andover
Hampshire
SP10 5BE
United Kingdom

Cengage Learning is a leading provider of customised learning solutions with office locations around the globe, including Singapore, the United Kingdom, Australia, Mexico, Brazil and Japan. Locate our local office at: **international.cengage.com/region**

Cengage Learning products are represented in Canada by Nelson Education, Ltd.

Visit Heinle online at **elt.heinle.com**
Visit our corporate website at **cengage.com**

Photo credits

The publishers would like to thank the following sources for permission to reproduce their copyright protected photographs:

Cover photo: Daniel Danilov (National Geographic Image Collection)

pp 2 (Shutterstock.com), 2 (Vincent J. Musi/National Geographic Image Collection), 2 (GazPatrick5/Istockphoto 3 (Shutterstock.com), 4 (Shutterstock.com), 5 (Shutterstock.com), 6 (Shutterstock.com), 7 (Shutterstock.com), 8 (Shutterstock.com), 9 (BLimages/Alamy), 9 (Shutterstock.com), 10 (Shutterstock.com), 11 (Shutterstock.com), 12 (Shutterstock.com), 13 (Shutterstock.com), 14 (Shutterstock.com), 16 (Shutterstock.com), 17 (Shutterstock.com), 17 (Shutterstock.com), 17 (Akiwi61/Dreamstime), 17 (ACHMAD IBRAHIM/APimages), 18 (Shutterstock.com), 18 (NASA/JPL/MSSS), 19 (Shutterstock.com), 20 (Shutterstock.com), 21 (Shutterstock.com), 24 (Shutterstock.com), 25 (Stephen Mallon/Gettyimages), 26 (Shutterstock.com), 26 (Joel Sartore/National Geographic Image Collection), 26 (Joel Sartore/National Geographic Image Collection), 26 (John Eastcott And Yva Momatiuk/National Geographic Image Collection), 26 (David Mclain/National Geographic Image Collection), 26 (Norbert Rosing/National Geographic Image Collection), 27 (Shutterstock.com), 27 (Shutterstock.com), 29 (Shutterstock.com), 32 (Shutterstock.com), 33 (Shutterstock.com), 34 (Vincent J. Musi/National Geographic Image Collection), 34 (Konrad Wothe/ Minden Pictures/National Geographic Image Collection), 34 (Flip Nicklin/Minden Pictures/National Geographic Image Collection), 35 (Shutterstock.com), 36 (LUCA BRUNO/APimages), 37 (Shutterstock.com), 40 (Shutterstock.com), 42 (Shutterstock.com), 42 (Bates Littlehales/National Geographic Image Collection), 42 (Beverly Joubert/National Geographic Image Collection), 42 (Karine Aigner/National Geographic Image Collection), 43 (Shutterstock.com), 44 (Shutterstock.com), 45 (Shutterstock.com), 48 (Shutterstock.com), 49 (Galina Barskaya/Bigstockphoto), 50 (GazPatrick5/Istockphoto), 51 (Roy Toft/National Geographic Image Collection), 51 (Michael S. Lewis/National Geographic Image Collection), 51 (Jason Edwards/National Geographic Image Collection), 51 (Jason Edwards/National Geographic Image Collection).

Illustrations by Katerina Chrysochloou

Printed by Seng Lee Press, Singapore
2 3 4 5 6 7 8 9 10 – 14 13 12 11 10